THE STORY OF
Maps

Written and Illustrated by **Terry Maloney**

F. R. A. S.

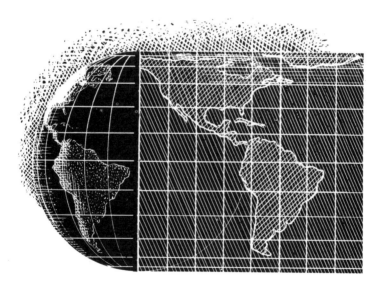

The Oak Tree Press

LONDON, MELBOURNE AND CAPE TOWN

Published in Great Britain and the Commonwealth in 1963 by
The Oak Tree Press Ltd.,
116 Baker Street, London, W. 1.

Printed in Great Britain by A. Quick & Co., Printers, Ltd.
Clacton-on-Sea, Essex.

CONTENTS

Sir Francis Drake commanded the first English ship to sail into
the Pacific. He was a skilful navigator and a bold pirate as well.

1. THE WORLD WAS ONCE A DISC

We are apt to take maps for granted nowadays. We feel confident, when we open an atlas, that what we see is a miniature version of the world. This was not always the case.

The fascinating story of maps goes back thousands of years. Even before history began, primitive man probably scratched crude maps in the dust. A few meaningful dots and lines, perhaps, would indicate how to find a certain cave, or an easy place to cross a river.

In ancient times, as civilization began, people thought the earth was flat. They imagined that the world was a large thick flat disc covered over by a circular heaven, to which the stars were fastened. That is what the Greeks thought three thousand years ago, although sometimes they drew a flat oval map of the world, just for a change.

Hecateus pictured the world as a disc in 520 B. C.

Maps which still exist from these early times reveal some interesting facts. The Greeks drew the world with their own country in the middle of the disc, in the Mediterranean Sea. The very name, Mediterranean, means "The middle of the earth." These ancient maps look queer to us, but to the Greeks they told a clear story about the entire world which was known *at that time*. A study of the story of maps shows how the ideas that men had in ancient times gradually changed.

2. TRAVELLING CAME BEFORE MAPS

The world of the Greeks was a very small one compared with the world we know today. To be sure, the ancient peoples were curious about what lay beyond their own frontiers, and most of them had legends about far-off places. They made up stories about places they had never seen to take the place of actual knowledge of what existed there, but their maps showed how small a portion of the earth they really knew. Today we study a map before we start to travel in order to find out where we're going, and the best way to get there. But in ancient times, travel came first. Only as men travelled and learned more about the real world could they draw maps which would be of real use to others.

The Greeks did not venture far outside the almost land-locked Mediterranean Sea, and with good reason. The kind of ships which they used made even a short voyage in the Mediterranean adventurous enough for most people. Their ships relied largely on the power of men's muscles. Some of their ships had sails, but they were fixed in one position. So they were no help unless the wind happened to be blowing in the direction in which they wished to travel.

This Greek galley was called a trireme, because the galley slaves rowed three banks of oars.

Such ships were hardly more than oversize rowboats, and almost completely at the mercy of the weather. Because of this, sea captains usually sailed by day and took shelter by night. They certainly didn't want to indulge in long trips away from land or well-known waters just for the fun of it. The time simply was not ripe for bold transocean voyages of exploration!

Just the same, although the world outside the Mediterranean remained more or less a mystery, there were plenty of people giving a good deal of thought to it. Thoughtful people wondered why the land seemed to drop off below the horizon as they sailed out to sea. And as they sailed towards land, they wondered why it seemed to rise gradually into full view. Perhaps the earth was not quite as flat as it was supposed to be!

3. THE WORLD GROWS ROUND

One of the people who believed in the roundness of the earth was a Greek named Eratosthenes, who lived in the third century B.C. He was the head librarian of the Greek-founded city of Alexandria, Egypt. Eratosthenes not only believed that the earth was round, but he accomplished a truly remarkable scientific feat. He worked out the actual size of the earth!

Up until that time no one had been able to do more than make vague guesses as to the size of the earth, but Eratosthenes managed to carry out this remarkable bit of work without anything in the way of modern instruments and without any complicated mathematics.

Eratosthenes started by measuring a shadow and ended up with a very accurate estimate of the earth's circumference. He reasoned that if you stuck a pole upright into the ground, no matter where, it would point directly towards the middle of the earth. If you had two poles a known distance apart and measured their shadows on the same day at the same time, the difference between the angle of their shadows would be the same as the angle at which the poles themselves would meet if they were long enough to reach to the middle of the earth.

Eratosthenes knew that on a particular day of the year at a place called Syene, the sun cast no shadow at midday. At midday on the same date he measured the angle of a shadow cast by a

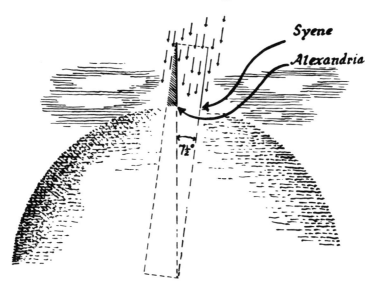

Without benefit of scientific instruments, Eratosthenes calculated the circumference of the earth with amazing accuracy. The shadow cast at Alexandria (the shaded portion) measured 7½° and therefore the angle between the two radii was also 7½°, because according to the geometry of Euclid, a straight line cuts two parallel lines at equal angles.

pole in Alexandria, known to be about 500 miles away. The angle proved to be about 7½°. There are 360° in a full circle (48 times as much as 7½°), and multiplying 500 miles by 48 to arrive at the sum of 24,000 miles for the earth's circumference was the easiest part of the job. That is very near indeed to the figure (24,840 miles) which more precise modern methods of measuring give.

People who believed, as Eratosthenes did, that the earth was round and knew of his estimate of the size of the earth must have wondered what existed in the rest of our vast world. Unfortunately, as we have seen, there were no seaworthy ships with which to explore, and no maps to guide the curious.

Strange as it may seem, about 500 years before the time of Eratosthenes, in the early 7th century B.C., great coastal voyages had been made by a seafaring people who lived at the eastern end of the Mediterranean. These were the same Phoenicians who gave us our alphabet. There is reason to believe that the Phoenicians actually journeyed all the way around Africa—through the Red Sea and down the east coast, around the Cape of Good Hope and back by way of the Straits of Gibraltar almost to their starting point. The Phoenician sailors brought back a story of having travelled through seas where the sun shone from the north! This tremendous voyage should have given people an inkling that the world was round, and an idea of its tremendous size, for the journey had taken several years.

Perhaps the strangest thing about this journey was the way it was ignored. A couple of centuries afterwards, the Greek historian Herodotus dismissed the "sun in the north" story as a typical wild tale of ignorant sailors! The epic voyage might never have been made for all the effect it had on maps.

4. THE MAP MAKERS' PROBLEM: ROUND WORLD, FLAT MAP

The fact that the earth was not, after all, like a plate but a ball of enormous size created new problems in map making. It meant that it was impossible to draw on a flat sheet of paper or parchment a completely accurate map of the world. You can prove this for yourself with paper and pencil, a ruler and a ball about the size of a tennis ball.

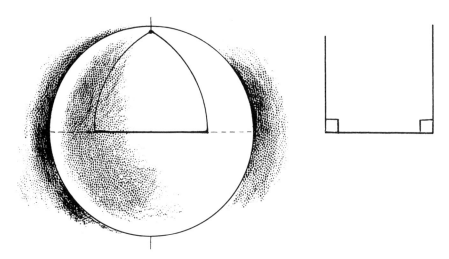

Draw an equator around your ball and then draw two perpendicular lines 3 inches apart and both on the same side of the equator. Continue drawing them until they meet, forming a triangle. Measure the length of the sides, and try to draw this triangle on paper, including the two right angles. As you can see, it is impossible to draw a triangle with two right angles in it. You can try the experiment again starting with an equator and one perpendicular line on your ball and then one more line to complete the triangle. Again, measure the sides of this triangle and then try to draw it on paper, including the right angle in the proper place. Can you do it?

On any flat map it is impossible to reproduce a large, straight-sided area whose corners have the same angles as they do on the earth's surface. *Any* flat map which shows a large portion of the earth's surface distorts the shape to some extent. The knowledge of the earth's true shape told geographers that the only way to draw an accurate map of the world was to draw it on a globe. Actually they began to do exactly that as early as 150 B.C., but roundness was almost the only feature of resemblance between these early efforts and the globes that we use nowadays.

Geographers were not the only people faced with the problem of trying to draw flat shapes to represent curved surfaces. Even before geographers ran into this problem it was an old one for astronomers. They had to map the "circular curve of the heavens," and had been doing it for years! Their maps of the sky helped to make possible more accurate maps of the ground and one of the most famous Alexandrian astronomers, named Ptolemy, became one of the most famous geographers and map makers as well.

He saw that the best way to fix the position of things on the ground was to do it according to the stars that passed overhead, and to use the same kind of network that the astronomers used. He pointed out that if several towns had a particular star pass directly overhead night after night it was because they were all at the same distance from the earth's equator. If the star was 20°

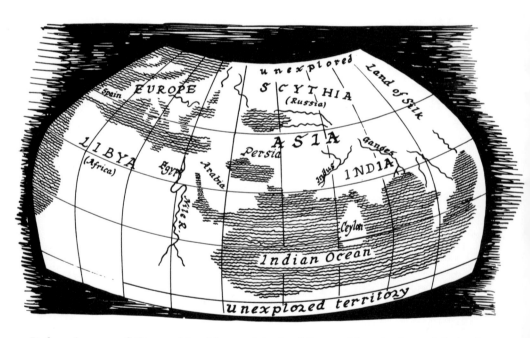

Ptolemy's map of the world with a network of lines of longitude and latitude. The Indian Ocean was an inland sea!

north of the "celestial equator," then the towns were 20° north of the *earth's* equator. Towns which had the same stars lying on their local north-south line (meridian) at the same time lay in the same *longitude.*

Lines like these already existed on star charts, but it was Ptolemy who brought them down from the sky.

As you can see, Ptolemy's map is very "modern-looking" compared with earlier maps. Even though mistakes are in it — the Indian Ocean, for example, appears as an inland sea — it is a great scientific advance over previous maps. There was no way of comparing different "local times" — no radio time signals and no accurate portable clocks. So Ptolemy made plenty of errors in longitude. But for hundreds of years all the best maps were based on his methods and his map of the known world was copied and recopied.

5. DARK AGES AND DIM MAPS

The Romans — who came after the Greeks — never achieved the high scientific level of Alexandria. They knew how to survey large sections of the countryside, and they made and used maps, but we know very little about them. No single original Roman map is known to have survived.

The six centuries which followed the fall of the Roman Empire (in 476 A.D.) were known as the Dark Ages, with good reason. As travel became rare between the countries which had been part of the empire, the flow and exchange of information and ideas which are necessary for scientific advancement came to a halt. In a sense, history went backwards, and much that had been discovered and known by earlier people was lost and forgotten.

Even the maps of this period suffered. Scarcely maps at all, they were far more primitive than most of the early Greek maps. Almost all of the learning was confined to the monasteries. Men of religion interpreted the Bible to mean that the earth was flat. They even included "Paradise" in some of their maps, placing it in the upper part of the map which to them represented the east.

This medieval T and O map showed an O-shaped world whose surface was divided up by a T. The segments were presented to the sons of Noah!

The simplest maps of this period were really primitive. Often called "T and O" maps because they resembled a letter T inside a letter O, they are known also as "wheel maps" because they show a round rim of ocean around a great mass of land divided into the three known continents, Europe, Asia and Africa. Some of the maps of the period, although more detailed, were wildly inaccurate.

While the T and O maps served no useful purpose, the Middle Ages produced another kind of map. This was a real traveller's map and was used to guide the Crusaders to the Holy Land. The "Route Map" was drawn in the form of a strip, often a very long strip, and was a direct descendent of old Roman maps. These maps showed all the places of importance along a particular route, but not the distances between them. Sometimes several roads, travelling in more or less the same direction, would be shown on a map as almost touching, although they might be a hundred or so miles apart.

14

LIONS HE ORE ABOUND
Media
ARABIA
Syria
Mesopotamia
Chaldea
Gog & Magog
Gad. Ruben
Upper Egypt
Mt. Olympus
ASIA MIN.
TROY
Lower Egypt
BRITAIN
SPAIN
PILLARS of HERCULES

The world of the Middle Ages when science was at its lowest ebb. The form of maps was determined by the artist's memory of other maps he had seen, accounts of travellers, facts of geography "that everyone knew to be true," and lastly, the actual shape of the piece of skin or wood that happened to be available for drawing on!

15

Maps like this were of use to the traveller only if he kept exactly to the route shown on the map. Very similar diagrams are still used today for certain purposes, such as to show the stations along a railway system. Sometimes rivers are mapped like this, with most of the deep bends smoothed out, and all the places of interest marked on the map. Such a map may be 6 feet long, but folded zig-zag fashion, it goes into an ordinary pocket quite comfortably.

6. THE AGE OF DISCOVERY: THE WORLD EXPANDS

In these days we often say, "The world is growing smaller," because of the increasing speed of travel and communication. Did you ever stop to think that for thousands of years, as new lands and new oceans were discovered, the world seemed to be getting steadily larger? Most exciting of all must have been the discoveries during the 15th and 16th centuries.

Perhaps you have wondered why so many of the discoveries of that time were made by Spanish and Portuguese explorers. The answer lies in the story of maps. It is a roundabout story which starts in Arabia, where the bright, clear night skies encouraged the study of astronomy.

As we have already seen, the study of the stars is important to the art of navigation, for even the best of maps are of little help in finding one's directions when there is no land in sight. The problem of moving across the deserts of Arabia and North Africa where sandstorms frequently erased all tracks on the ground was not very different from that of navigating the seas. Travellers needed to know how to take their directions from the sky. And so, during the long centuries while western Europe slept like a bear in its cave, the Arabs made use of the lessons taught by Eratosthenes and Ptolemy.

In the 8th century the Arabs invaded and occupied the Iberian Peninsula (Spain and Portugal). When they finally withdrew a few centuries later they left behind a great store of knowledge of astronomy and the art of navigation, and also many practical improvements in the rigging and handling of ships. So it was that those two countries had a head start in the race into the unknown, and that is why we find so many Spanish and Portuguese names in the list of famous explorers — Vasco da Gama, Ponce de Leon, Magellan, and of course Columbus, who, although Italian, sailed for Queen Isabella of Spain.

The "stately" *Santa Maria* of Columbus must have seemed far from stately to those aboard her as she heaved and rolled in seas whose habits of storm and calm were as unknown as the coasts she hoped to reach.

We know now, it is true, that earlier Europeans, the Norsemen, from Scandinavia and Iceland had sailed to Greenland and North America. In the 8th century Norse sailors had crossed the Atlantic to Labrador and had even gone inland. However, the only reason we know of their voyages is from evidence discovered recently in America itself. As to their methods of navigation we know nothing.

In a sense, the Norsemen did not really discover America because they brought back no maps to inform other peoples about it. But the great voyages of Spanish and Portuguese explorers transformed maps for all time.

Imagine what it must have been like during the exciting period when all of maritime (sea-going) Europe was wondering what prizes lay beyond the distant horizon. People at that time thought

When Magellan's speck of a ship passed through the stormy straits which bear his name, he entered a region completely unmapped. He opened up a new era. Although Magellan himself died on a Pacific island before the momentous journey was completed, his courageous crew completed the first circumnavigation of our globe.

their ships had reached a high level of perfection. They were large enough to carry large stores of food, and their sails were able to take advantage of winds from any quarter. With favourable weather they could sail quickly enough to encourage an attempt to cross the great ocean.

Part of a map drawn in 1669, this drawing shows how much more was known about the coastal areas, which were settled, than the interior, which wasn't. This was true of most maps of America.

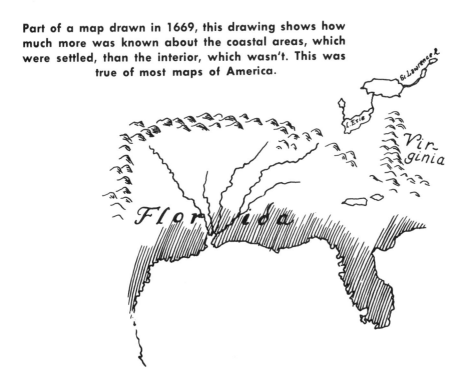

Many educated people realized the hugeness of the earth's surface, and knew what a small part of it was occupied by the continents of Europe, Asia and Africa. To them it seemed unquestionable that over on the other side of the ocean there must be one or more continents to "balance" the northern land-masses of the known world. In addition, they hoped to be able to reach the great "silklands" of the Orient, the source of silks and spices and all sorts of other riches, by journeying westward around the globe.

As for the southern regions below the equator, some thought they were "fiery" and uninhabitable, while others thought a warm sunny climate encouraged the growth of gold.

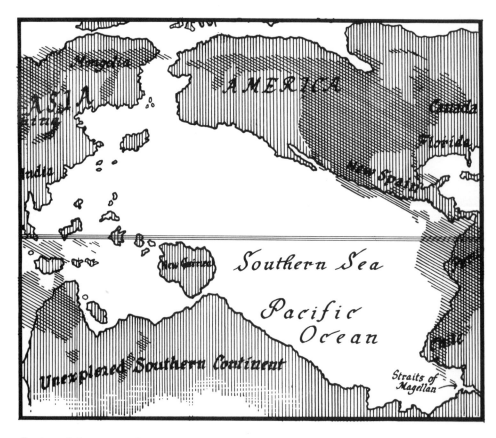

Fact and fancy combined in this late 15th century map which was amazingly good in some respects and completely wrong in others. Until precise time-keeping at sea made accuracy possible, estimates of positions in longitude were often wildly at fault, so that east-west positions or distances were distorted. Notice that the vast imaginary southern continent which drew men into the badly-charted Pacific Ocean is drawn with almost as much detail as the non-imaginary west coast of America!

The first complete journey around the earth by Magellan's expedition in the early 16th century, along with Columbus' famous voyage to the New World, answered many questions—and raised others. Following, as it did, da Gama's voyages down the coast of Africa across the equator, it proved that men were able to survive the crossing of the "fiery regions," and also proved that the route around the globe to the Orient was a long one.

Wise men urged European kings to fit out expeditions to reap the harvest of precious things in a great continent, still undiscovered, away off to the south—not South America, but a land south of there. The Straits of Magellan were thought to separate the southern tip of South America from that land, and for many long years sailors returned with stories of peaks of land which they had sighted there, which they would surely have reached "except for unfavourable winds"!

That imaginary "Great Southern Continent" existed on maps for many years. We have already seen how the map of Ptolemy showed a southern continent joining Africa and Asia. However, after ships began to sail into the Indian Ocean from the Atlantic, the "Terra Australis Incognita" (Latin for "Unknown Southern Land") had to be moved or abandoned altogether.

One of the things about early maps that you will notice is that the men who drew them were not very fond of empty space. If no one knew what lay in a particular region, they would often complete it according to their own fancy. The gaps in many maps were filled in with illustrations of famous voyages. Fish and sea monsters filled the oceans, while the supposed wind directions were often shown as windbags or humans representing the winds, puffing air into the sails of ships.

Here is a strangely compressed Africa whose unvisited interior gave plenty of scope to lively minds. Ropelike mountain chains and astonishing rivers indicate a dislike of empty and unused drawing space as much as they represent any real attempt to illustrate the tales of natives and travellers. The child sitting by the shore has a single eye in the middle of his forehead. Land monsters of this kind were popular inhabitants of unfamiliar lands.

This actual 16th century map lists the cities alphabetically as well as showing their positions. A terrible storm is breaking up the unfortunate ship on the right.

The period of exploration and discovery in the 16th century brought about a new interest in geography as well as a new need for accurate maps. People wanted to see the record of voyages of such navigators as Magellan and Columbus and the other great sailors who first opened up the world to their wondering gaze. For the map maker, it was a period of constant revision and addition. New maps were hardly published before fresh discoveries made them out of date!

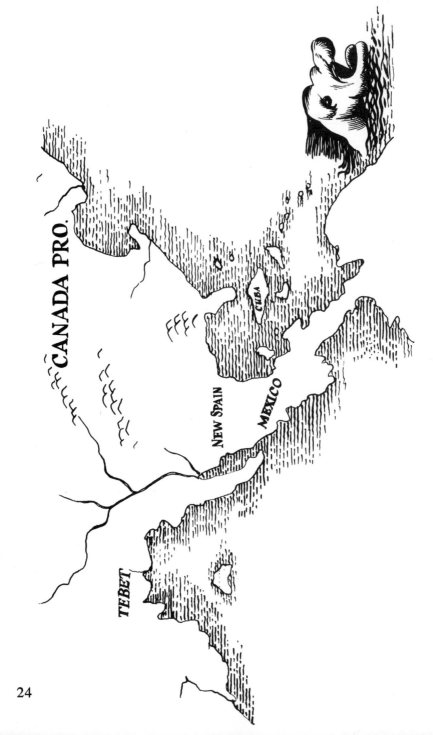

CANADA PRO.

TEBET

NEW SPAIN

MEXICO

CUBA

In this map Asia and North America are one continent, sharing a river which evidently serves as a boundary between them.

These maps, amusing as they may seem today, are more than mere drawings. The information they gave was often faulty, but they show the growing science of map making, and tell a story of the courage of the men who made them possible.

We know today the true size of the oceans as those men did not. Men sailed off into the unknown in small sailing vessels which today we would hardly consider seaworthy. Despite the constant threat of tempest and the danger of death due to disease, they brought back bit by bit the information which changed the entire conception of the globe.

This map, while made in the late 16th century, is certainly a close relative of today's modern maps. The general shape of America is recognizable, but its position is misplaced in relation to the rest of the world. This error was due to the difficulty the navigators had in those days of knowing their east-west position (longitude) accurately.

Mariners were able to estimate their north-south position (latitude) quite accurately by means of the astrolabe. This instrument, invented by Arabian astronomers, was used to measure the angle of the sun or a fixed star much as Eratosthenes had measured the angle of the sun to find out the size of the earth. But there was no simple and effective way of finding how far east or west a ship

Globes were made by geographers as early as 150 B.C. This is a reconstruction
of a 16th century globe depicting new discoveries. Although the "Great
Southern Continent" which is so prominent turned out to be a dream, its
northern coastline bears a real resemblance to the Australian coast, and was
probably not entirely guesswork.

had travelled without some accurate means of keeping the time.
Clocks would not work at all in a choppy sea, and even on shore
they did not keep correct time.

7. MERCATOR THROWS AWAY THE NORTH AND SOUTH POLES

Because of the uncertainty concerning longitude, navigators had to rely not simply on their maps and charts, but on experience. Compass reading, once it was learned, became a valuable piece of knowledge. This 16th century map — covered with compass direc-

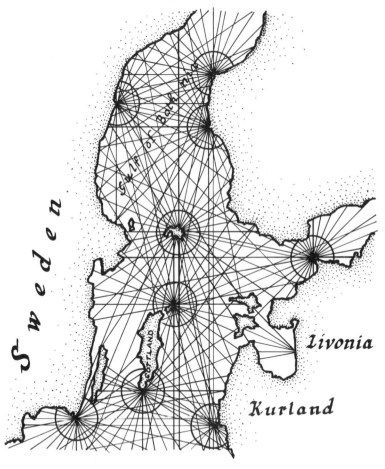

This is how the Baltic sea looked in a 16th century map with straight lines connecting all the places where a captain might want to sail. He merely chose the line which would take him from where he was to where he wanted to go and set his compass accordingly.

The compass "rose" was more than a decoration on old maps. Often it was lovingly embellished with national devices like this one with the fleur-de-lys because it was a tie with home. To be sure, the compass was not always reliable, but its mysterious north-seeking finger enabled men to cross oceans whose true size was unknown to them.

tions — shows how important the compass was becoming. These compass bearings were useful on charts of small areas like the Baltic; they could not be applied to world maps of the time.

But the compass bearings provided the germ of an idea that was soon going to make all charts out of date.

In the late 16th century a Flemish geographer named Mercator invented a world map with one important purpose: to give mariners accurate compass directions. Instead of drawing the meridians (lines of longitude) as converging curves meeting at the poles, he drew them as parallel straight lines. And then he drew the parallels of latitude further and further apart as they got further from the equator to match the extra space between the meridians at the top and bottom of the map.

On Mercator's projection of the world, you can tell at a glance the compass course that would take a ship from any place on earth to any other place. There are no poles because on Mercator's map the meridians never meet.

29

However, no one at the time was the least bit interested in sailing to the poles, or even to the far north. Losing the poles, and having the far northern lands distorted out of all proportion to the lands near the equator, was a cheap price to pay for the convenience of accurate directions.

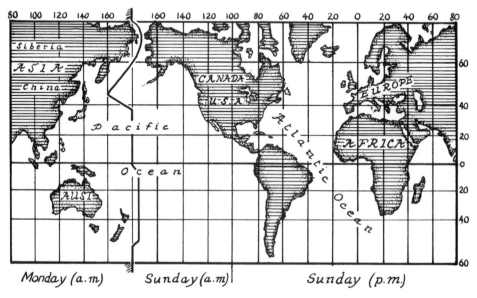

Map of the world based on Mercator's projection with the heavy meridian indicating the International Date Line.

This "working map" was a big success and was soon used by all navigators. It provided the charts on which all the later voyages of exploration were based.

8. CAPTAIN COOK FINISHES THE JIGSAW PUZZLE

Even when the wonders of the New World had ceased to be big important news and American colonies had been established to take their place in the pattern of civilization, people still hankered after the elusive Southern Continent. By then it was pretty clear that the southern hemisphere had some enormous stretches of ocean, but could it be so covered with water as to exclude the Great Southern Continent altogether? What about all the sailors' reports that they had seen it, and even visited it?

From time to time the search was renewed. Penetration of the southwest Pacific by the Dutch had brought many new names to the map: Van Dieman's Land, New Holland, the Tasman Sea. Further to the north lay the great island of New Guinea which for

Australia was almost the last stronghold of ignorance among map makers. When they weren't sure, they improvised. Here they attached New Guinea to Australia.

Captain James Cook was a mathematician and astronomer as well as a navigator, explorer and geographer. He was also a physician who discovered that it was possible to keep men at sea for long periods of time without deaths from scurvy by giving them fresh fruits or vegetables instead of the hardtack and dried meat which had been the standard diet up until then.

a long time appeared on maps as part of the Australian mainland. But no one was able to find the elusive Southern Continent.

Not until the 18th century was the mystery finally solved, by the greatest navigator of them all, Captain James Cook.

Cook was an Englishman and his voyages were altogether different from Columbus' journeys three hundred years before. Columbus was a discoverer; Cook was a scientific explorer. His expeditions consisted of systematically sweeping back and forth through the Antarctic region of the Pacific. He established once and for all that the Great Southern Continent was a myth. The land which had been a lure for so long was realized to be, at best, a bitterly cold desert of ice, much smaller and much closer to the south pole than had been imagined.

Cook was the first ship's captain to have the benefit of accurate timekeeping instruments, making precise measurement of positions in longitude possible. It showed what glaring errors had been made in the past. Cook tried to visit islands listed by earlier voyagers as significant discoveries. He could find no trace of them!

The area surveyed under Cook was enormous. Whole stretches of the Australian and New Zealand coasts were charted. A final search for the long-sought northern passage from Europe to India convinced Cook that mariners had been pursuing a mirage. There was no such passage. As a result of Cook's thorough explorations, it became possible to draw a map showing most of the surface of the earth as known territory, in which it would be pointless to search for any land except perhaps small islands.

From Cook's time onward, it remained only to fill in the gaps.

California temporarily became an island. This is part of the same map shown on page 19.

The outlines on the map became the same outlines that we find on our maps today. The great rivers rising in Asia and flowing through America which we can find on earlier maps were no longer possible. The mythical "Lands of Gold," regions of "One-Eyed People," countries of midgets, or giants, or monsters, became a thing of the past, and maps became accurate records of observed and verifiable fact.

9. MODERN MAPS WITH A PURPOSE

Accuracy has long been the goal of map makers, but the old problem of what kind of accuracy to strive for in a map remains. The world is still round and maps are still flat.

Once the map maker knows the purpose for which his map is intended, he can make it as accurate as possible in that particular feature. We have already seen how Mercator handled one problem. He retained accuracy of a single feature—compass direction—knowing that the distortion of shapes and sizes would not interfere with his map's usefulness for navigators.

(On next page) ⟶

Before we can draw the outlines on a map or a globe, we must first draw a network of lines to guide us. Let's start with a ball on a string or axis. First we start the ball spinning in the direction of the arrow (upper left). Next (upper right) we hold a paint brush at the midway point and as the ball spins it draws the equator which divides the globe into the northern and southern hemispheres. Now we stop the ball and draw a perpendicular to the equator. We continue this line or meridian around the globe, dividing it into eastern and western hemispheres (left centre). Then we look at it obliquely from above the north pole (right centre). Now we are ready to add horizontal lines. We do that by placing dots at equal intervals along the meridian (bottom left). Now when we spin the globe the dots extend around in the parallel lines of latitude (bottom right).

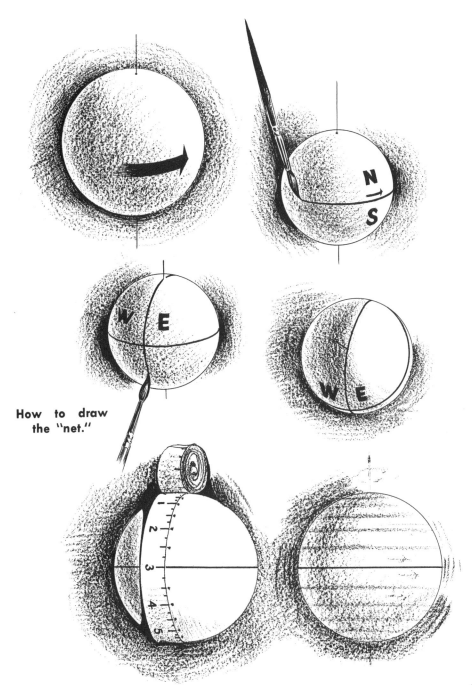

How to draw
the "net."

If the map maker is content to show only a small part of the earth's surface, rather than the entire world, he can be much less drastic. He can draw the area he wishes to present with a reasonable degree of accuracy in all respects. For instance, a narrow area that lies along the equator can be drawn by almost any method of charting. Both direction and scale will be constant enough for *shape* and *area* to be reasonably accurate. Most maps only tell one kind of truth. Either they tell the truth about direction, or distance, or area. They cannot tell the *whole* truth about the *whole world* at the same time, on the same map!

We start with a transparent globe of the earth with the lines of longitude and latitude printed on its surface.

If we want a map that shows the *areas* of the different countries of the entire world true to scale there are several ways of doing it. This kind of map is useful when we want to compare the sizes of land masses or oceans, the density of peoples or the distribution of natural resources, etc.

As with all maps, we have to start by producing the network of lines of longitude and latitude (the net) and these must be set down in such a way that the areas enclosed by the various "strands" of the net are in proportion to the same areas on the globe. One way of doing this, the easiest, is shown here.

We start with an imaginary transparent globe which already has the lines of latitude and longitude printed on it. We place it, north pole down, inside a transparent imaginary hemisphere of twice the diameter of the globe. A projection lamp placed exactly at the south pole will now project these lines onto the half-ball. If we now stand the half-ball on paper, we can project the new set of lines onto the paper by moving our projection lamp so that it is in line with the two poles — but at an "infinite distance."

In this final projection, the dot in the middle is one pole, the equator is the heaviest of the circular lines, while the other pole is the line all around the edge! We could now fill in the outlines of the continents on this grid (another name for the net). Although

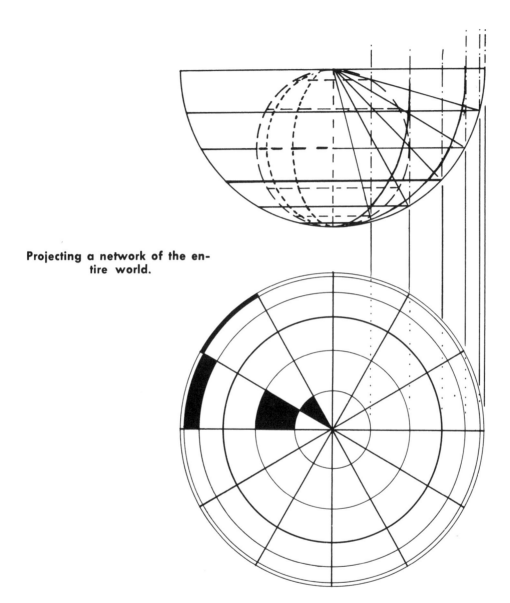

Projecting a network of the entire world.

the *areas* would be accurate, the shapes would be extremely distorted near the edges of this map as you can see from the blackened portions of the drawing. Added together, the two at the edge are the same area as the two at the middle, but on the real world they

37

are also the same shape. You would never suspect this from looking at the drawing. As in the case of most special maps, it is good for the one purpose but useless for others. The outer portions of the map would be too misshapen to be of any practical use, although this is quite a good map for dealing with the polar regions by themselves.

There are far better "projections" for equal-area treatment of the whole globe. By "splitting" the globe part way towards the equator before we project it on a sheet of paper we can avoid all the worst distortions and still keep to the truth concerning size. But a "divided" or "re-centred" map of this sort must not be used to find out the direction of one place from another.

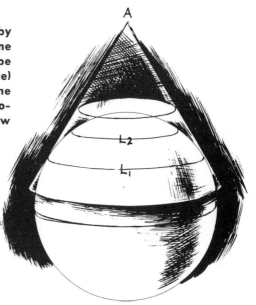

Part of the globe is covered by a cone. The apex of the cone which extends beyond the globe is removed (left, opposite page) and the remainder of the cone is opened and spread flat. Notice that lines L_1 and L_2 are now curved instead of parallel.

Here we see another type of projection. The *conical projection* supposes a piece of paper rolled into the form of a cone and placed over the globe. After the projection of the shadow lines from the

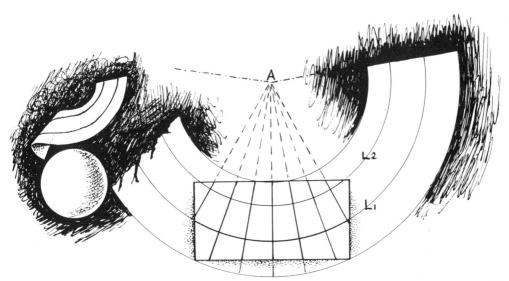

globe onto the paper, the paper is "opened out" and the part required is used. If you look at an atlas you will see that the net used varies according to the location of the country concerned. Countries like the United States will often have a net like that in the right-hand drawing. Countries which straddle the equator would never be drawn on this network.

A cylindrical projection is the kind of map we would get by wrapping a cylinder of paper around the globe. Mercator used a

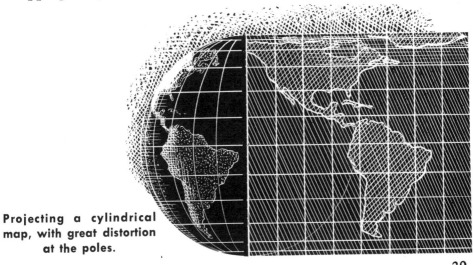

Projecting a cylindrical map, with great distortion at the poles.

"modified" cylinder. A true cylindrical projection shows areas in their true relative sizes, which Mercator's does not, but the shape of the polar regions is very distorted and the whole thing looks terribly squashed. The use of such a map is very limited.

If we want to show the shortest route between any two places on the map as a straight line we use a *gnomonic* projection. This is the view of the network of lines from a point at the exact middle of the inside of the globe. You cannot make a gnomonic map of the whole world. On a gnomonic map you cannot tell the *distance*

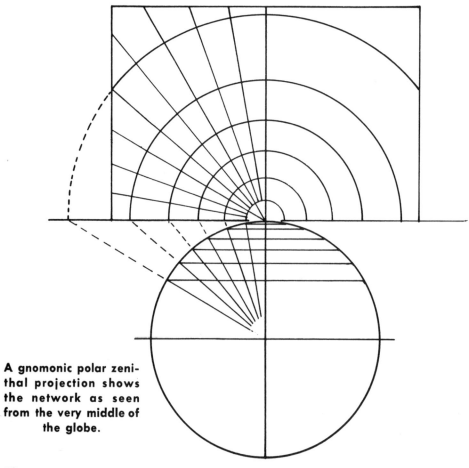

A gnomonic polar zenithal projection shows the network as seen from the very middle of the globe.

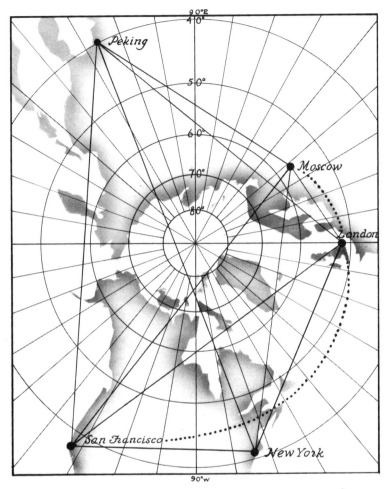

The shortest distance between two points is a straight line on this map. Compare with the map on the next page.

of the straight line which represents the shortest route except along the equator, or directly north-south on the map's "central meridian." If you use the gnomonic map alongside another map giving better scale, you can easily transfer the line to the second map by connecting the corresponding points through which it passes. On the second map, the shortest actual route becomes a curve, corresponding to the curve of the earth's surface.

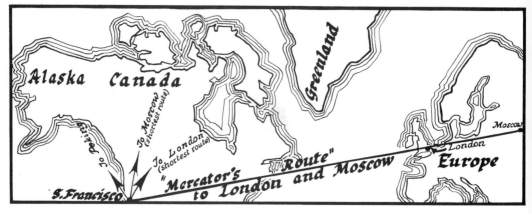

This drawing is based on Mercator's projection of the world. The heavy line shows the best route from San Francisco to London and Moscow according to this map. Compare this with the small arrows showing the routes that are actually shortest, and then look at the map on page 41. The dotted line on *that* map is the exact route you would follow if you took the straight line on Mercator's map.

Map makers in this age of flight have been faced with a new version of an old problem — a navigators' map showing true direction as well as the shortest route by air. On the azimuthal equidistant map of the air you can plot the shortest distance from the **middle** of the map by means of a straight line drawn on the map. Since the concentric circles on the map are drawn to a known scale, the straight line will tell actual distance as well as direction. The odd-looking map here is centred on Tokyo, and on it you can quickly find the shortest route from Tokyo to any place on earth. If you are used to thinking of directions in terms of the "ordinary" or Mercator projection of the world, you will be in for a few surprises. For instance, if you plot a course between Tokyo and Newfoundland on this map, you will find that you fly north, almost over the north pole, instead of flying in the eastward direction which appears to be the most direct route according to Mercator's map.

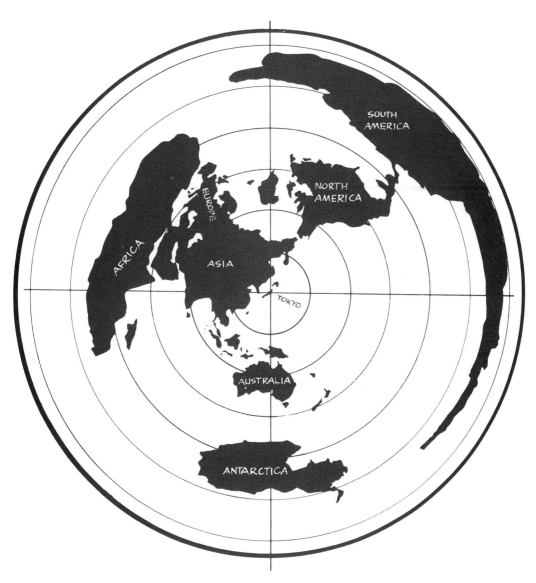

This azimuthal equidistant projection, centred on Tokyo, is fairly accurate for the area which is near Japan. The farther we go towards the edge, the greater the distortion grows. South America has been so spread out sideways that it looks like a crab, and the thick line around the very outside represents the antipodes of Tokyo—that is, the dot on the opposite side of the world from Tokyo.

The following map is drawn with London as its middle. Remember that an azimuthal projection can only be used to plot a course from its middle.

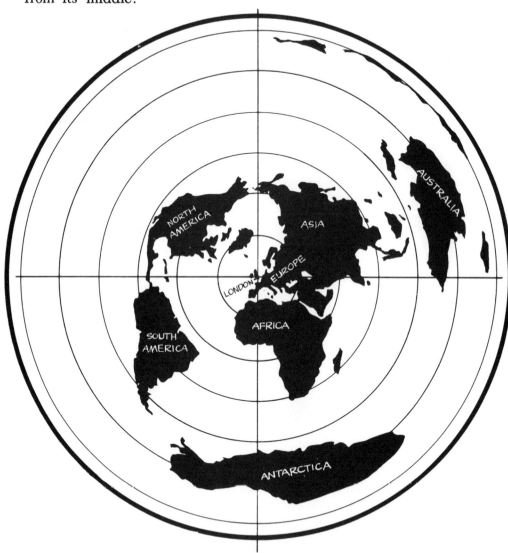

On this map most of the continents, though distorted, are still recognizable. The straight lines on the map, incidentally, are the true north-south and east-west lines for London.

These are truly maps of the air age, so new and revolutionary that to many people they look as queer as the ancient maps with their distorted shapes and sizes. In a sense we have come full circle, and these maps, like the first one in this book, make the world look like a disc. But the air map is a disc without a horizon, and it encompasses the entire globe. It achieves its special accuracy of direction and distance, paradoxically enough, by means of the most extreme inaccuracy. Look, for example, at that long mass along the outermost circle of the map centred on Tokyo. It is South America!

The entire map is contained within a border which on the surface of the earth is a mere point. The whole edge of the map is actually a point—the point on the far side of the world from the spot at the middle!

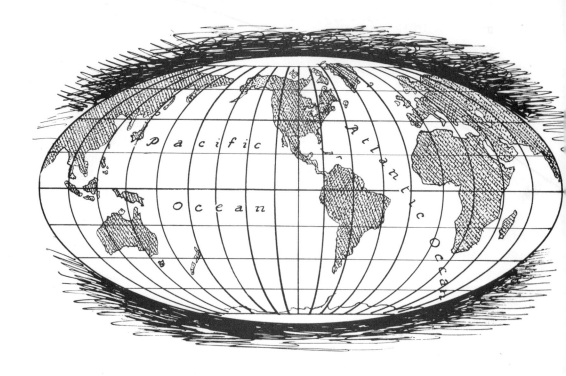

This may look like a Japanese lantern, but it is another modern map of the world. Mollweide's projection is another method of reducing our round globe to a flat piece of paper. There is less distortion in the polar regions than Mercator's projection and equal areas are maintained.

The making of a map net for any *polar* projection — gnomonic, stereoscopic, equidistant, involves only one problem, the spacing of the parallels. The meridians are simply marked off with dividers or protractor at their true angles and at the desired intervals.

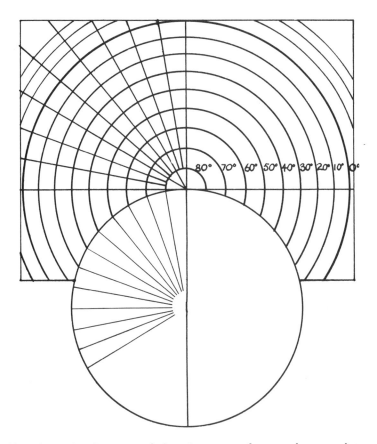

Here is a simpler way of drawing a net for a polar equal-area map. It will provide reasonably true shape for Canada, Alaska, Northern Russia and Scandinavia. Beyond the Equator (heavy line at 0°) countries would look squashed.

One of the easiest and most useful is the "minimum error" map "projected" in the same manner as shown in these examples, but with the projection point outside the globe.

This sketch of North and South America is based on Mollweide's projection, showing the true proportions of the areas drawn. The inset shows Alaska as it would appear on a Mercator's projection of the world—drawn to the same scale at the equator!